SIGNS OF HEALTH

SIGNS OF HEALTH

A Pocket Medical
Sign Language Guide

CATH SMITH

Illustrations by Cath Smith

CO-SIGN COMMUNICATIONS

First published 1999 Reprinted 2010
ISBN-10: 0953506916
ISBN-13: 978-0953506910

Published by Co-Sign Communications,
(Incorporating Deafsign & DeafBooks.co.uk)
Stockton-on-Tees

Tel: 01642 580505   email: cath@deafsign.com
www.deafsign.com   www.DeafBooks.co.uk

Distributed by Gardners Books
1 Whittle Drive, Eastbourne, East Sussex, BN23 6QH
www.gardners.com   Tel: +44 (0) 1323 521777

Printed in Great Britain by Stephen Smith
email: admin@deafbooks1.co.uk
Tel: 0191 4274 665 Fax: 0191 4274 599

Dedicated to

The Deaf Community of Teesside

ACKNOWLEDGEMENTS

My grateful thanks and appreciation to;

'The Consultants' who contributed their knowledge and expertise in sign language and deafness to the making of this book; Tony Beckett, Anita Duffy, Craig Jones, and Sandra Teasdale, and for making the process enjoyable.

To Robert Riley and Stephen Smith of Alphabet Press for their moral support, their patience and for hours of computer time, and to Joanne Dunn for her Fingerspelling illustrations.

To Susan Stones, RGN RM Dip Nursing and Sheila Robson BSc (Hons) RN RM Dip Nursing FETC Cert H Ed, for their professional advice.

To Doug, Lyn and all the staff of The Forest Bookshop, for their vision and hard work.

To Peter Moon, for his advice and assistance in the preparation of this publication.

And as always, a big thank you to my family, and to Mum and Dad whom I miss very much.

CONTENTS

INTRODUCTION

Deaf people in health care and medical settings

Imagine you are taken ill or suffer an accident in a country where you do not speak the language. Picture the situation of trying to explain how it feels, what the symptoms are like, give a history, and to understand the instructions and questions of those who are doing their best to find out what's wrong and treat you, but just can't understand what you are saying. Just imagine waking from an anaesthetic to discover parts of your anatomy missing, like your breast or your testicles. This chilling prospect can be a reality in the lives of people who are deaf.

One of the most critical areas of life in which human communication is literally vital, is in the field of health and medicine, yet, as this book explains, deaf people face severe barriers to communication unless special steps are taken. This publication is aimed at breaking down such barriers and improving communication.

PASSIVE DISCRIMINATION

Direct experience with deaf people in medical settings, as elsewhere in society, brings home the paucity of awareness of deaf people's communication needs, faced on a daily basis throughout their lives. Although not intended or deliberate, even passive discrimination due to lack of knowledge and understanding, is oppressive and potentially dangerous.

Misunderstandings and bad experiences can happen to anybody, but it doesn't take too much imagination to realise that deaf people are at a distinct disadvantage when it comes to giving and receiving information such as may be involved in diagnosis and preparation for treatment, or even in acquiring the simple day to day knowledge relating to the body and health matters that the rest of us take for granted. There are examples of good practice, but unfortunately these are few and far between. As we approach the 21st century, horror stories still abound of fear, confusion, uncertainty and inadequate preparation for major procedures, which can can no longer be considered acceptable.

Not only is deafness invisible, but its profound effects on the individual require time, effort and imagination to fully appreciate, and this is not an easy task in the busy lives of hospitals and other health care environments. There are growing numbers of medical professionals attending sign language and deaf awareness courses, and this is encouraging, but it can be difficult to maintain skills, particularly in sign language, when real-life face to face contact with Deaf* patients is irregular. Although there is a massive 8.7 million people with a hearing loss in this country, the incidence of deafness from birth or infancy is low (approximately 1 per 1000 of the population), making the need for reference material even more important. A hospital midwife comments;

> *"I come across barriers to communication from time to time, one of these being communication with Deaf people. This can result in misunderstandings about care given and received if we are unable to communicate effectively … a book aimed at all those involved in the health care field would not only prove a valuable aid, but would also encourage us to learn more about sign language. This will also prove useful to the Deaf community either in hospital or at the local surgery."*

A small book such as this can only scratch the surface, but is intended as a quick and easy to use

* The convention of the upper case 'D' in *Deaf* refers to people who identify themselves as culturally Deaf sign language users.

reference guide that is accessible to busy professionals under pressure. This may lead to better understanding in the immediate situation, and offer encouragement to go on and learn more. It is **not** intended to replace the need for skilled communicators and interpreters, but offers practical information to improve communication and is relevant to all people with a hearing loss.

DEAFNESS AND HEARING LOSS

Deafness is an all-embracing term that means different things to different people. It can occur at any age and may vary in degree from slight to severe or total. The onset of deafness may be sudden or gradual and may be linked to other conditions such as vertigo, tinnitus or visual impairment. Deafness may be caused by illness, injury or hereditary factors and may or may not be treatable – the effects can be as varied and individual as we are ourselves.

However, it is useful to try and identify two broad and separate groups of deaf individuals for whom the effects of deafness are fundamentally different in terms of **identity and communication**. The implications of deafness from birth or infancy are different from those of deafness occurring later, the most crucial factor being language and cultural identity.

There are over eight and a half million people in Britain with a degree of hearing loss that interferes with everyday life and communication. Within this figure are about 56,000 who are deaf from birth or early childhood, for whom spoken language is largely inaccessible, and whose main link to language, and to the world, is visual.

The majority of people with hearing loss — the bulk of the 8.7 million referred to, are those who have developed or acquired hearing loss during their lives, **after** childhood and spoken language development. They have developed as 'hearing' people and spoken language will continue to be their inner language even though they may no longer be able to hear it. The lesser figure of 56,000 of born deaf people for whom English (or other spoken language) is not their first natural language in either its written or spoken form, make up Britain's Deaf sign language community. Although much of the information in this book will have relevance to both groups, the sign language using Deaf community is its main focus.

EFFECTS OF DEAFNESS ON LANGUAGE DEVELOPMENT

The situation for children deaf from birth or infancy presents an unusual paradox from a language point of view, in that, for most families, there is a mismatch between the child's language needs and the language of the home, that is not always readily appreciated or understood.

There seems to be a general assumption that deaf children who can't hear speech will develop sign language, or become skilled speakers and lip-readers, by some magical, if unknown, process. In reality, about 90% of deaf children are born into hearing families, who are unlikely to know anything about deafness or sign language, at least in the early years after diagnosis. A high proportion of these – as much as 81% has been quoted – never learn to communicate effectively with their children.

For a variety of reasons, deafness may not be diagnosed until the child fails to develop spoken language, so that special steps such as hearing aids, sign language, the understanding of deafness and so on, may be absent during the vital early language learning years, with serious life-long consequences of delayed and limited language development for all but the lucky few. The 10% or so of deaf children born to Deaf parents, and those who receive adequate language input in the early years, tend to fare much better linguistically.

The situation is further clouded by the fact that the education of deaf children is a minefield of controversial issues concerning communication and language teaching methodologies in which the individual's needs may or may not be met.

As a result of all these factors, many adult Deaf people do not acquire English as a first natural language and will have limited access to written information.

National studies of reading in most countries of the world confirm deaf children's average performance when leaving school to be similar to that of 9 year-old hearing children. The situation for profoundly deaf children is even bleaker with nearly 50% not reading for meaning at all.

The majority of people deaf from birth or infancy communicate in British Sign Language, with varying degrees of ability in English in either its spoken or written form. In spite of this, Deaf people **do** have a lifetime's experience of communicating with the hearing world and rely mostly on lip-reading and writing for their day to day exchanges.

Clearly, there are situations that require the services of sign language interpreters or other communicators of the Deaf person's choice.

ABOUT BRITISH SIGN LANGUAGE

British Sign Language (BSL) is the language of Britain's Deaf Community for whom it is **essential** and highly **valued**. It has a history of repression by educationalists, but, because of deaf children's need for visual language, its use has never diminished. Sign languages flourish all over the world, wherever Deaf people come together, but although they share common structures and elements, they are not all the same language.

In Britain, there is wide variation in sign vocabulary, the 'words' of the language, that can be compared to accent and dialect in spoken language. This is not a problem for Deaf people, since it is the grammatical structures that are the main vehicle of meaning.

Sign language is visual and gestural, it uses a different medium to the spoken, auditory medium that hearing people are used to. This different medium brings with it certain restrictions and at the same time certain possibilities and advantages that we may not be expecting. Put simply, sign language is structured differently to spoken language, in ways not immediately obvious. A common observation of sign language is that it appears 'brief', or incomplete. This is explained by the fact that sign language is less 'word' based than spoken language, and uses particular ways of integrating detail into signs in an economical way so that although production is slow compared to the speed that words can be spoken, there is no loss of meaning.

The components of BSL that allow this to happen are the specific handshapes, three dimensional use of space, the location and orientation of signs within that space and the speed, direction and type of movement. These are combined with non-manual information carried by the head, face and body.

All of these factors can be taken in by the eye at the **same time**, so that what looks like one sign can be loaded with detail such as intensity, frequency, negation, and of who did what and with which and to whom, giving far more than a sign to word equivalent. By compressing more detail into the signs themselves, messages can be put across that would need a lot of words to deliver. This may sound complicated, and is, in fact a complex area, but sign language classes and other teaching resources do help to make these things clearer, offering practical and detailed examples. **SIGNS OF HEALTH** is an introduction to some of these ideas that might whet the appetite for more.

A WORD OF CAUTION: MIND YOUR LANGUAGE

Many health care practitioners are aware of the importance of modifying language and medical jargon for the benefit of patients and lay people generally, but it is worth stressing here how crucial this can be for Deaf people, and that extra care needs to be taken.

Because of limited access to information, Deaf people's understanding of commonly held knowledge of basic bodily functions, malfunctions and treatments cannot be taken for granted. Some examples that Deaf people may have problems with are; *allergy, antibiotic, benign, malignant, cardiac, HRT, paediatric*, and so on, words that we can usually assume to be generally understood. If an interpreter is present, then of course, it is their job to convey the message in intelligible terms, but there will be occasions when you are on your own, and you will need to be inventive and use your imagination.

Some are easier to deal with than others, *paediatric* for example can be conveyed by signing *children's* (*doctor, ward, treatment*, or whatever, according to the context) whereas others, like *anti-biotic* may prove difficult. Producing a sign, or fingerspelling a word does not guarantee it will be understood.

SENSE AND SENSIBILITY

In addition, Deaf culture brings with it a different perspective and sometimes different sensibilities, so that things that may be regarded as taboo, or offensive in the hearing world are not regarded as such in the deaf world and vice versa. The terms used to describe parts of the body and bodily functions give an example of this.

Many Deaf people do not use words like *penis, testicles, vagina, urine, faeces, rectum*, and so on, but use signs with accompanying lip-pattern or fingerspellings such as *cock, balls, fanny, shit, bum* (even taboo words like *cunt* may crop up as just another term for a bodily part), which may appear unexpectedly from sweet little old ladies in the surgery.

In the hearing world, these words may not be considered appropriate in a 'formal' setting like a medical consultation, even though commonly used elsewhere, but the same restrictions don't necessarily correlate in the deaf world. Deaf people may also be unfamiliar with the many euphemisms used in this area, which hearing people often employ as alternatives to the 'correct' or medical terms. There are no hard and fast rules however, and there is wide variation in these matters.

(The glosses or "headings" for the signs illustrated in this book give the more formal variety, since the book is primarily aimed at non-Deaf readers).

The Deaf world also has rules of behaviour and manners, for example it is considered rude for hearing people to talk among themselves without signing or without trying to include the Deaf people present, or to stand in the way of Deaf people signing to each other.

DEAF PEOPLE'S EXPERIENCES

In an attempt to put a human face to some of the issues involved, two real life examples of Deaf people's experiences follow (translated from BSL).

"I went to see my sister (Deaf) in hospital just after her operation and she was hysterical. Her husband (Deaf) was trying to pacify her, but she was so upset. She had come round from the anaesthetic to discover that her breast had been removed and she had no idea that that might happen — no preparation. I didn't know what to do or say, she was distraught and so were we. She died not long after, and that memory stays with me."

This example happened several years ago, but similar experiences still occur.

However, there are also incidences of good practice, as the following example shows;

> *"So I went with my husband to see the specialist about a vasectomy. The doctor was very good and explained everything very carefully — drawing pictures, diagrams of the tubes and everything, and asked us if we wanted to ask any questions, but it was quite clear and understandable. The operation was straightforward and my husband went to the Deaf club the same night."*

In the **Deaf Women's Health Project** carried out by Judith M. Collins, Deaf Studies Research Unit, University of Durham, it was found that in medical consultations, approximately 65% of Deaf women go on their own and communicate by writing or speech, even though these women would prefer to communicate in sign language.

It was also found that generally Deaf women do not get enough information and do not have the information communicated to them in a way they can understand.

Research by the Royal National Institute for Deaf People (RNID) reveals that GPs across the country are inadvertently risking the lives of patients who are deaf or hard of hearing simply because they do not know how to communicate with them.

Their survey, **Breaking the Sound Barrier,** uncovered disturbing statistics detailing the huge problems deaf and hard of hearing people face when visiting their GP.

For many people the situation is so bad they have given up visiting their doctor when they are ill, staying at home with potentially life-threatening conditions. Worse still, nearly a quarter of those who do see their GP leave the surgery still not knowing what is wrong with them. RNID Chief Executive, James Strachan commented,

> *"As a deaf person myself I am shocked but not totally surprised by the extent of the problem. It is outrageous to think that a deaf or hard of hearing person receives a lower standard of primary health care simply because of their hearing loss ... The real irony is that, when it comes to communication, only a small amount of effort makes a world of difference ... "*

MAKING A DIFFERENCE:
COMMUNICATING VISUALLY

For Deaf people whose main link to the world is visual, (in addition to the millions of people who are hard of hearing), there are numerous practical ways of improving communication and making life more comfortable. This is by no means an exhaustive list, but the following pointers can make a difference;

Be aware that deaf people rely on vision and will be alert to all the **non-verbal** cues that we give out automatically and have little control over. Visual cues – **facial expressions, gestures** and so on – make up a massive percentage of what we communicate. A grim expression, or a twinkle in the eye, will cross any language barrier, and natural body language expressions of concern and reassurance speak louder than words.

Eye contact. Communication cannot take place unless the Deaf person is looking at you. Try to avoid moving around as you speak, or talking with your head down as you write. Hold things up for viewing or point to things when necessary. Give people time to look at what you are pointing at, then back at you.

Good lighting. Deaf people need to be able to see clearly.   To assist lip-reading, the light should be on the speaker's face.

To further help **lipreading**, speak a little slower, but in a natural rhythm without exaggeration. Keep the message straightforward and clear, and if there is difficulty, try saying it another way.

Be aware that a response of **smiling and nodding** may just be an automatic response and does not necessarily mean that the message has been understood.

Always have **paper and pen** ready to write things down. English may not be the Deaf patient's first language, so keep the message simple and direct.

A good way of attracting a Deaf person's attention is by **flashing the lights** on and off several times. **Tapping** the arm or shoulder is another way of gaining attention.

Strong sunlight, or other bright lights can make things difficult, particularly for Deaf people with additional eye conditions like Retinitis Pigmentosa, (approximately 5% of Deaf people have **Usher Syndrome**, combining congenital deafness with Retinitis Pigmentosa).

Eye drops may also affect vision, and patients need to be warned beforehand. Any procedure in which the eyes must be closed (e.g. EEG) or in which the patient is out of eye contact (e.g. during an X-ray), also need instructions to be given beforehand.

A procedure such as an MRI scan can be quite frightening when cut off from all contact, and this needs to be fully explained before the procedure starts. Even people who normally manage well with hearing aids will be cut off in this situation.

If an **interpreter or communicator** is being used, allow several seconds time lag for the message to be interpreted.

A number of hospital and health centre waiting rooms use ticket number systems with **visual displays** to indicate a patient's turn, which are far more appropriate for people with hearing loss than calling the patient's name.

Deaf people as in-patients may be able to benefit from the use of **teletext television** and **subtitles,** and **text telephones**, such as minicoms. It is also useful if wards keep supplies of hearing aid batteries. Loneliness and isolation, not to mention sheer boredom, are frequently experienced by deaf people in hospital.

SIGN LANGUAGE INTERPRETERS
AND COMMUNICATORS

Deaf people may choose to have a sign language interpreter with them during consultations, and it is useful to have some understanding of the interpreter's role and code of practice.

There is a national Register of Sign Language Interpreters and Communicators, regulated by the Council for the Advancement of Communication with Deaf People, based in Durham (see **Useful Addresses** section at the back of this book).

The Council also publish a Directory of Interpreters and Communicators with details for contact and availability. There is a shortage of interpreters nationally and bookings need to be made well in advance, and availability cannot be guaranteed. Professional interpreters are bound by a code of ethics requiring impartiality and confidentiality.

Many Deaf people prefer to be with a family member, or a close friend or social worker, even if their communication skills are more basic. It seems that trust and confidence in their 'interpreter' matter more to Deaf people than just language skills, and it is important that Deaf people have a choice in these matters.

ABOUT THIS BOOK

This book is split into two distinct parts; the illustrated **SIGN VOCABULARY**, which gives an alphabetical collection of signs for quick and easy reference, particularly useful for urgent or emergency situations, and the **DIY SELF-ASSEMBLY FLAT-PACK** section on sign 'invention' designed to encourage learners to understand Deaf people's creations and make up their own on the spot as the need arises.

Hospitals and other health care settings have their own specialist terminology and vocabulary that can intimidate even the most articulate patient. It would be unrealistic to try to provide sign vocabulary for all potential procedures, treatments, equipment and medical conditions across the numerous and diverse disciplines in medicine.

In addition, this book is intended to support and improve better awareness of deaf people's plight and to encourage better everyday communication, rather than for medical staff attempting to 'interpret' in crucial situations where professional (or other) interpreters at Deaf people's request should be involved.

Learning sign vocabulary is only one small part of getting to grips with sign language, and real life interactions may prove baffling without some basic understanding of the processes at work.

Researchers refer to signs such as those shown in the illustrated 'dictionary' section of the book as fixed, or **established** vocabulary. These are comparable to the words of spoken language, and are invaluable in expressing the everyday exchanges that accompany hospital life – words that relate to daily routine, comfort, procedures, visiting etc.

For this reason, the signs chosen include basic 'core' vocabulary in addition to some of the more specialised signs.

Attempts have been made to include signs that are widely used and understood, and details of alternative variations of signs are also given when space allows. Where possible, details are also given that will clarify a sign's meaning in context, and on facial and bodily expression essential to the sign's production, or that can change its meaning.

GUIDE TO HEADINGS AND CAPTIONS

Languages have very few direct word for word equivalents between each other, and the headings given for each sign are a guide to meaning rather than a direct translation. Where possible, more than one word heading is given, to give a clearer idea of its context.

The captions are intended to give extra information on the handshape, location and movement of signs, as well as additional details of variation, changes in context and details of facial and bodily expression when relevant and where space allows.

Signs and fingerspelling are described and illustrated as if the signer is right-handed, with the right hand always referred to as R. and the left hand as L.

Left-handed signers will use the reverse of this, with the left hand as dominant.

From the thumb, the fingers are referred to as index, middle, ring and little finger.

DIRECTION, ORIENTATION AND MOVEMENT

Terms used to describe the direction in which the hands face, point or move are given here.

Description of hand orientation is based on the direction in which the palm faces regardless of whether the hand is open or closed.

As illustrated here, the R. hand is palm left and the L. hand is palm right, or they can also be described as palm facing, or palm in.

The hand may be described as 'pointing' up, forward etc., even if the fingers are bent in a different direction or closed.

As illustrated, both hands are pointing forward, palms facing.

Diagonal movements are described 'forward/left' or 'back/right' and so on.

Some signs start with a full description of handshape and position before movement is made. This is then called a **formation**, which means they keep their position together as they move.

BASIC HANDSHAPES

Closed Hand	Flat Hand	Clawed Hand	Fist

Bent Hand	Bunched hand	'C' Hand	'M' Hand

Full 'C' Hand	Full 'O' Hand	Irish 'T' Hand	Bent 'V' Hand

'N' Hand	'Y' Hand	'O' Hand	Open Hand

'V' Hand

These are frequently used handshapes in BSL and the terms used in this book to describe them. If the handshapes are described for example as *index, middle finger and thumb extended*, then it is understood that the other fingers are closed.

31

ARROWS

Repeated movement

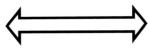

Movement in one direction
then the other

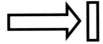

Movement ends with
stress

Hands move apart

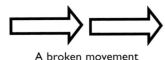

A broken movement

Open hand closes

Small repeated movements
or wiggling

Closed hand opens

Impact on point drawn

Some signs show the
starting and **finishing**
position of the hands,
usually in a lighter and
darker line.

32

SIGN VOCABULARY

Illustrated lexicon

ACCIDENT

Fingerspell letter 'A', then R. hand forms 'C' and makes two small hops to the right. May vary e.g. R. clawed hand shakes back and forth near side of head (see also *mistake, sorry*).

AFTER/WARDS

Palm down R. closed hand with thumb out is behind L. flat hand, then twists in small forward arc over L. Can be R. hand only. See also *later*.

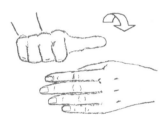

AFTERNOON

Fingertips of 'N' hand touch side of chin, then twist to point forward. Can be two 'N' hands pointing inwards, then tips of R. hand brush forward against tips of L. (regional).

AGAIN, REPEAT

R. 'V' hand is held with palm facing left and fingers pointing forward/up. Hand shakes forward/down from wrist. Also means *frequently, often.*

AGE, HOW OLD?

Fingers of palm back open hand wiggle in front of nose. With raised or furrowed eyebrows in question form, means *how old? what age?*

AGREE, CONSENT

Two 'good' hands move in towards each other, so that knuckles touch. The head nods and lips are pressed together. Also means *appropriate, suit, suitable.*

36

ALLERGIC, ALLERGY
Tips of bent fingers rub up and down forearm in agitated movement, teeth clenched (also *itchy*). Symptoms vary, but this is a generic sign. **May need explanation**.

ALWAYS, REGULAR
Knuckles of R. 'good' hand brush left to right along L. palm. Also means *normal, ordinary, usual, usually.*

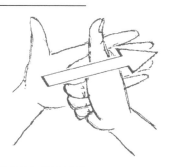

AMBULANCE
Fingers of full 'O' hand spring open as hand revolves in circles. May vary, e.g. tip of R. index or thumb makes cross on left upper arm (also *hospital*, or *nurse* in some areas).

37

ANAESTHETIC, GAS

R clawed hand is held palm back in front of nose (also **gas and air**). May be signed as **injection** as eyes close and head tilts to one side.

ANALYSE, INVESTIGATE

Palm down 'V' hands with fingers pointing in, move slightly apart, twice, as extended fingers flex. Also means **examine, research**.

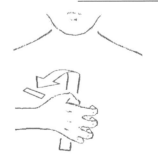

ANGRY, FURIOUS, MAD

Clawed hand moves sharply up chest, twisting to palm up (brows furrowed, and cheeks puffed). Both hands may be used. Movement may be alternate (**frustration**).

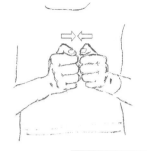

APPOINTMENT

Closed hands move in towards each other, so that knuckles touch. May tap together twice. Also means **book, booking**.

ASK, ENQUIRE

'O' hand moves forward from near mouth (as in *I'll ask*) or 'O' hand is held forward and moves back to signer (as in *ask me*). May change in context. Directional.

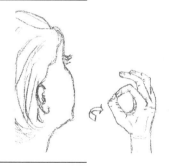

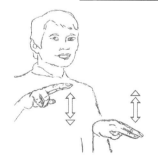

ASSESS/MENT, TRIAL

Palm down 'N' hands move up and down alternately. Flat hands can be used and may be palm up or palm down. Also means **evaluate, judge,** and similar meanings.

BABY, INFANT

Fingers of palm up R. flat hand rest on fingers of palm up L. flat hand as hands rock slightly side to side. Can also be small up and down movement or other variation.

BAD, AWFUL, SERIOUS

Closed hand with little finger extended makes small movement (can be forward, back or side to side), with negative facial/bodily expression. Both hands can be used for extra emphasis.

BATH

Closed hands rub up and down on chest several times. Flat hands can be used. For *bed-bath*, or *wash*, a flat hand is moved across the body in washing action.

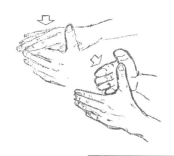

BECAUSE

L. flat hand is held palm facing right with thumb up; fingers of R. flat hand move down onto edge of L. index, then back onto inside of L. thumb. See also *why? reason.*

BED, SLEEP

Head tilts onto palm of flat hand. Can be both hands held together palm to palm. With eyes closed, also means *sleep* (see also illustration *sleep*).

BEDPAN

Full 'C' hands pointing down with palms facing back, move out and apart and twist round in outline shape of bedpan. People and objects can also be referred to by pointing.

41

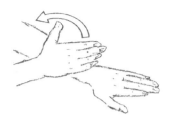

BEFORE, PRIOR

Edge of R. flat hand moves up left forearm in small arc or with repeated brushing movements (also *early*, *premature*). Means *before* as in "*before* you go home." May vary.

BEFORE, IN THE PAST

Palm back flat hand makes small movements backwards near the shoulder. Means *before* as in "have you had this problem *before*?" or "did this happen *previously*?"

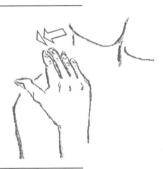

BETTER, IMPROVE

Tip of R. extended thumb makes small repeated brushing movement against tip of L. extended thumb. Single sharp movement means *best*. See also entry for *improve*.

BIRTH, BORN, DELIVER

Palm up flat hands held at sides of the waist move forward and in towards each other. May vary, e.g. fists twist downward in pushing movement in front of body (regional).

BLANKET, BEDCLOTHES

Palm back fists make firm movement up front of body. Can be signed with fists palm up in front of body moving up/back onto chest.

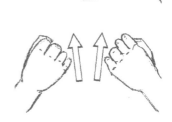

BLOOD, BLEED

R. open hand brushes forward/down across back of L. open hand. Fingers of R. hand may wiggle, also meaning **bleeding.** See also entry for **period**, **menstruation**.

43

BLOOD SAMPLE

Backs of fingers of R. 'V' hand contact left arm; hand moves forward and away from arm as extended fingers close onto thumb. Can also mean **take blood,** or **aspirate, drain,** etc.

BLOOD PRESSURE

R. hand briefly grasps left upper arm, then opens and closes in squeezing action. Can be followed by palm down flat hand moving up, or down (**high** or **low blood pressure**).

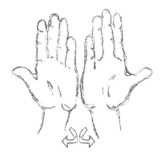

BOOK, READ

Flat hands held palms together, swivel open like a book. Formation makes small side to side movements in front of the face, for **read** and **study**. See also entry for **read**.

BORED, BORING

Fingers of flat hand tap against chin twice, the mouth is slightly open in an air of boredom. Also means *dull*, *tedious* and similar meanings.

BOWEL MOVEMENT

Flat hands, palms facing down/back, brush alternately downwards on lower abdomen several times. Fast repeated movements for *diarrhoea, runs,* etc. May vary.

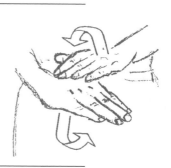

BOY, LAD

Thumb and index finger holding end of chin, brush down closing together. May repeat. Varies regionally e.g. R. index points and brushes left on chin, or tips of 'N' hand brush chin.

45

BREAK, FRACTURE

Palm down fists held together, twists sharply to palm up and apart in action of snapping (for *fracture*, specific part of the body may be indicated by pointing).

BREAK, RELAX, REST

Thumb tips of palm down open hands touch chest. Head may tilt to one side. Fingers may wiggle. Also means *comfortable*. Hands flop downwards for *relax*, *respite*.

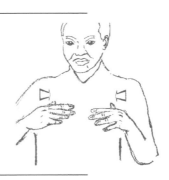

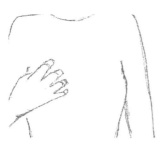

BREAST

Tips of clawed hand are held on side of chest, or flat hand taps side of the upper chest. Sometimes indicated by cupped hand making outline shape on chest. Both hands for *breasts*.

CAN, ABLE, COULD

Index finger of palm back 'C' hand flexes as it moves forward/down from nose (may flex repeatedly a few times). May start on forehead. Also means *ability*, *possible* and so on.

CAN'T, COULDN'T

Extended index finger moves down looping over in crossing out action, as the head shakes (with negative facial expression). Both hands may be used, (also *impossible*, *unable*).

CARE, CAREFUL/LY

Extended index finger moves forward/down from near eye as it flexes. Both hands may be used. Also means *take care*, *be careful*.

47

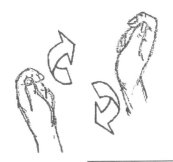

CHANGE, ALTER
Irish 'T' hands held with palms facing, twist over and cross at wrists. Handshape and direction may vary in context., e.g. upright index fingers swap places as in "*change places.*"

CHANGE OF MIND
Middle finger tip of 'V' hand touches forehead, then hand twists to palm forward, and tip of index finger contacts forehead. May repeat. Also means *work out*.

CHECK, EXAMINE
R. index finger points to eye, then 'Y' hands move downwards in quick twisting movements from the wrist. One hand only may be used. Also means *check up inspect*, *test*, and so on.

CHILD

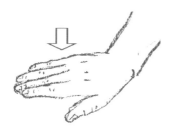

Flat hand makes short movement down in front of body. Upward movement at head height for *adult.* Movement is repeated to the side several times for *children.*

CLEAN, CLEAR

R. flat hand sweeps forward/right along L. hand. Can also be signed with edge of R. flat hand brushing twice along L. palm. *To clean* is signed differently in different context.

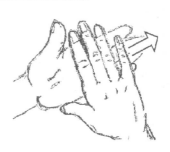

COCHLEAR IMPLANT

Tips of bent 'V' hand touch the head behind the ear. Different types of implants would be located on the appropriate part of the body.

COFFEE

'C' hand makes several very short quick twisting movements near side of mouth. May be signed with R. fist on top of L. fist in grinding movement.

COLD, SHIVERY

Clenched fists make several short movements towards each other. Elbows are tucked in and the shoulders hunched, with cheeks puffed. Also means *chilly, winter, wintry.*

COMMUNICATE

'C' hands move alternately backwards and forwards in front of body. Palm up flat hands may also be used, also meaning *correspond, deal with, negotiate* and similar meanings.

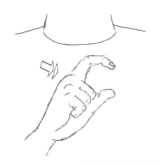

COMFORTABLE, CONFIDENT

'C' hand taps front of chest twice. Shoulders move slightly up and down alternately. Hand moves up or down body slightly for **gain** or **lose confidence**.

COMPLAIN, MOAN

Clawed hand makes small upward brushing movements on chest twisting to palm up. Face and body show negative feeling. Also means **grumble, whinge** and similar meanings.

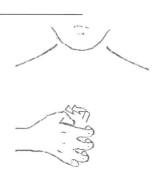

CONFIDENTIAL

Open hands held apart near chin, move inwards in firm grasping movement, closing to form fists, one on top of the other in front of mouth. See also **private**.

51

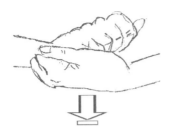

CONSTIPATED, BLOCKED

Closed hands crossed at wrists, held on lower abdomen, make short firm movement down. Can be two fists, one above the other in same location, pulling into body.

CONTACT, JOIN, CONNECT

Hands move together and form two 'O' hands that interlink. If hands then move backwards and forwards, the meaning is *relate*, *relation*.

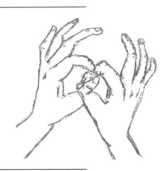

COUGH

Index edge of fist bangs against chest twice.

COUNSEL, CONSULT

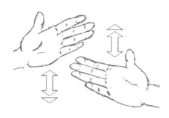

Palm up flat hands move backwards and forwards alternately several times. Also means *converse*, *discuss*, *negotiate*.

CURTAINS

Irish 'T' hands, palms facing inwards, move towards each other at head height. Can be one hand only, and move in direction appropriate to context.

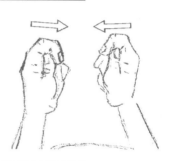

CUT, SCISSORS, SNIP

Index and middle fingers open and close as hand makes small movement forwards. Downward movement near groin often used to indicate *vasectomy* (both hands).

DANGER, DANGEROUS

Index edge of R. flat hand taps forehead twice, or may make single sharp movement. See also *risk, risky*.

DAY, LIGHT

Palm back flat hands held crossed in front of face, swing upwards and apart. **Day** is also commonly fingerspelt.

DEAD, DIE, DYING

'N' hands are held pointing up, with palms facing, then twist from wrists to point forward (slow movement for **dying**).

54

DEAF, DEAF PERSON

Tips of extend fingers of 'N' hand touch the ear. If cheeks are puffed, the meaning is **profoundly deaf, really deaf.**

DEPRESSED, SAD

Slightly bent hand brushes down chest. Mouth is turned down and shoulders sag. Also means **feel low**, and similar meanings. With lip-pattern "phew" also means **relief**.

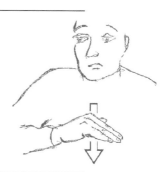

DIAGNOSE, DETECT

Extended L. index finger held forward, R. clawed hand grasps shut, as it moves forward to contact back of L. index. Also means **diagnosis**, **identify**.

DIFFERENT
Index fingers held together with palms facing down, move apart as they twist over to palm up.

DINNER, MEAL
Palm back 'N' hands move up to mouth alternately. Sometimes signed with R. 'N' hand edge down on L. 'N' hand, making small cutting action.

DIRT, DIRTY, UNCLEAN
R. open hand rubs in small anticlockwise circles on palm of L. open hand. The nose may be wrinkled, or other negative expression.

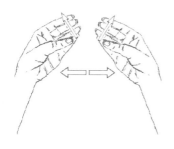

DISSOLVE, MELT

Thumbs rub along pads of fingers from little fingers to indexes, as hands move apart. In different contexts also means *cure*, *solve*.

DIZZY, SPIN, VERTIGO

Index touches forehead, then makes small horizontal circles at side of head. Sometimes signed with palm back open hand circling face. Body may sway slightly.

DOCTOR, MEDICAL

R. middle finger and thumb tips 'hold' L. wrist and tap twice (with no movement, means *pulse*). Index and thumb can be used. See also *medical*. *GP* can be fingerspelt.

DON'T KNOW

Tips of palm back flat hand touch forehead, then hand swings forward/down to finish palm up. The head shakes and shoulders lift slightly.

DON'T LIKE, DISLIKE

Flat hand brushes up middle of chest in single emphatic movement, moving away and twisting to palm up as head shakes. Nose may be wrinkled, brows furrowed.

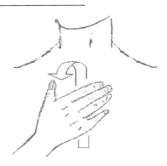

DON'T WANT

Open hand brushes up side of chest in single movement, moving away from body as it twists to palm up. The head shakes with negative expression.

DRINK, GLASS

Full 'C' hand moves up to mouth with small tipping movement.

DRIP

Index finger flicks downwards off thumb several times.

DRUG, DRUGS

Thumb closes onto index and middle fingers in action of using hypodermic syringe on left arm. May be repeated, and used as generic sign for **drugs, drug abuse**.

59

DRY

The thumb rubs across pads of fingers from little finger to index. Both hands can be used moving apart meaning *dried up*, or *dissolved* and related meanings.

EAT, FOOD

Bunched hand moves towards mouth in small repeated movement. Also used for *breakfast*, *lunch* and *supper*.

ENJOY, HAPPY

Flat hands make repeated brushing movements against each other and face shows positive expression. Also means *delighted*, *pleased* and similar meanings.

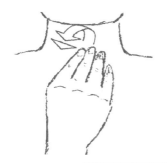

ENOUGH, PLENTY

Fingers of palm back bent hand brush forward/upwards twice against under side of chin. Also means *adequate*.

EQUIPMENT, MACHINE/RY

Palm back clawed hands swivel from wrists towards each other so that fingers interlock. Also means *technology* and similar meanings.

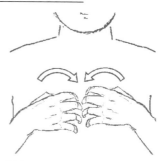

FALL, COLLAPSE

R. 'V' hand (used here as legs classifier) 'stands' on L. palm (also meaning *stand*), then twists over to land on L. palm. Also means *fall over, faint*.

61

FAMILY

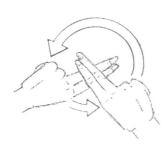

Hands in fingerspelt 'F' formation move in small horizontal circle. Sometimes a palm down open hand is used in same movement.

FATHER

The R. fingers of fingerspelt 'F' formation tap the backs of L. fingers twice. Sometimes used for **dad**, **daddy**.

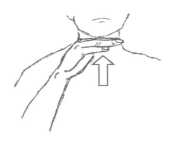

FED UP, HAD ENOUGH

Back of bent hand moves firmly up to contact underside of chin, with negative expression. May tap twice. With neutral expression, means **full up**.

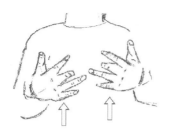

FEEL, FEELINGS

Hands move upwards with tips of middle fingers brushing chest. One hand only may be used. Also means *emotions* and similar meanings.

FINGERSPELL, SPELL

Fingers and thumbs of both hands wiggle against each other as hands move to the right. This refers to the British two-handed system.

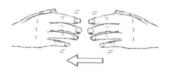

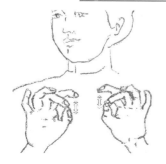

FINISH, FINISHED

Middle finger tips tap repeatedly against thumb tips. One hand may be used. Also means *completed* and similar meanings. One of several variations.

FORCEPS DELIVERY

Palm facing bent 'V' hands twist slightly inwards and move back towards body in small pulling movement.

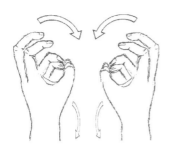

FRIEND

R. hand clasps L. in short up and down shaking movement.

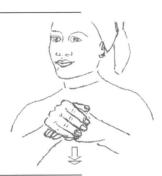

GIRL, FEMALE, WOMAN

Index extended from closed hand, palm forward, makes small repeated forward brushing movement across cheek.

GIVE, GAVE, PASS

Palm up flat hands move forward in a context such as "*I gave*," or back to signer as in "*give me*." Can be one hand and handshape may vary. As drawn also means *let*.

GOOD, GREAT

Closed hand with thumb up makes small movement forward. Both hands can be used. Commonly used in greeting as *hello*, or with raised brows as question *all right*?

HARD, DIFFICULT, PROBLEM

Tip of R. thumb prods the centre of the L. palm twice.

HEARING PERSON

Extended index moves from ear to chin. May tap against chin twice. The thumb is sometimes used instead of index finger.

HEART ATTACK

Index fingers make two short jabs towards each other, on left side of chest. Can be located on different parts of the body, meaning *sharp pain*, or on forehead, *headache*.

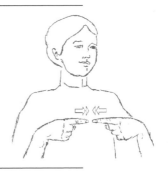

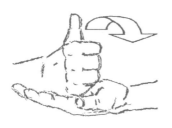

HELP, ASSIST

R. closed hand with thumb up rests on L. palm. Hands move forward in a context such as "*I'll help*," or back to signer as in "*help me*."

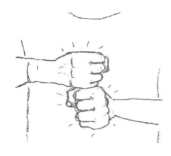

HOLD YOUR BREATH

Fists held one above the other on the chest pull back into body. If located on lower abdomen, can be used to mean **constipated**, or to indicate holding on to either urine, or faeces.

HOME, GO HOME

Hand held up with palm facing forward swings in forward arc to finish palm down.

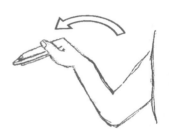

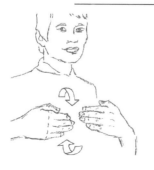

HOSPITAL

Palm back flat hands revolve forward round each other several times (R. hand only revolving round L. gives **bandage**). Can be index or thumb making cross on upper arm (regional).

67

HOT, HEAT

R. clawed hand with palm facing backwards, moves sharply across the mouth from left to right.

HOUSE, HOME

Extended fingers of 'N' hands touch at an angle then move down/apart in outline shape of building. Flat hands are also sometimes used.

HURT, PAINFUL, SORE

Open hands shake floppily from wrists, up and down alternately (may be one hand only), with pained expression. Also means *injure*, *suffer* and related meanings.

HUSBAND, WIFE

Thumb and finger of R. hand make short repeated movement along upper L. ring finger. Also means *spouse*, *ring*.

ILL, ILLNESS, UNWELL

Edges of extended little fingers brush downwards on chest (can be one hand only). With slow movement and cheeks puffed, head to one side, the meaning is *tired*, *worn-out*.

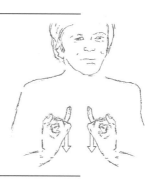

IMPORTANT, TOP

Palm down L. flat hand moves down onto tip of extended R. index finger. May tap twice. Also means *crucial*, *vital*.

IMPROVE, IMPROVEMENT

Tips of index and thumb of R. 'O' hand move upwards along upright L. index finger.

INFECTION

Edges of extended little fingers tap twice against upper chest. Repeated fingerspelt initial 'I' also sometimes used, and other variations.

INJECTION

Thumb closes onto index and middle fingers in action of using hypodermic syringe. Can be located on appropriate part of anatomy.

INTERPRET, INTERPRETER

Upright 'V' hands twist backwards and forwards alternately from the wrists several times. 'N' hands are also sometimes used.

KNOW

Tip of extended thumb moves up to touch forehead. May tap twice. Head may nod.

LATER, AFTER

Upright index moves in small arc to the right, bending from the wrist. May make small repeated movement.

LAY, LIE DOWN

Back of R. 'V' hand (legs classifier) moves along length of L. palm to end of fingers.

LIGHT, LAMP

Fingers of full 'O' hand spring open. This would be appropriate for **light on** (open hand closes for **light off**). Can be located and directed to suit context.

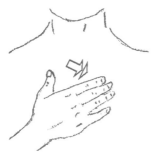

LIKE, FOND OF

Flat hand taps twice against upper chest, with appropriate facial expression.

LIPREAD
'V' hand with fingers bent makes small circular movements in front of the mouth. Also means **lip-pattern**.

LIST, PROCEDURE
R. closed hand with thumb extended and pointing to the left, moves down from L. palm with small twisting movements from the wrist. Also means **order**, **sequence**.

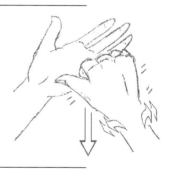

LIVE, ALIVE, LIFE
Tip of middle finger makes small up and down rubbing movements on side of upper chest.

LOOK, WATCH

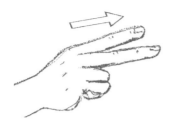

Fingers of 'V' hand move forward from near eye, or move/point in direction to suit context. Two 'V' hands point towards each other for **eye contact**.

LUMP

R. index finger makes outline of lump on left arm, or can be located on the appropriate part of the body.

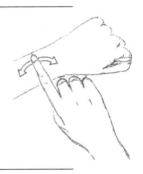

MAN, MALE

Hand holds and strokes downwards on chin with thumb closing onto fingers. May vary e.g. index finger edge of R. full 'C' hand on chin; hand moves forward closing sharply to a fist.

MAYBE, MIGHT, PERHAPS

'Y' hand makes small quick twisting movements from the wrist, or palm up flat hands move up and down alternately (***possibly***, ***uncertain***). The lips are stretched, head tilted.

MEDICAL

Index edges of two full 'O' hands contact chest several times as they move down the body simultaneously. There are a number of variations of this sign, see entry for ***doctor***.

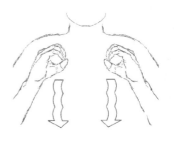

MEDICAL, DOCTOR

Tips of bunched hand contact left, then right side of chest. An 'O' hand can also be used. There are a number of variations of this sign, see above.

MENINGITIS

Fingers of R. 'M' hand tap twice against side of lower skull. May vary, e.g. tips of clawed hand tap against side of neck (*stiff neck*).

MINE, MY, MY OWN

Closed hand moves back to touch chest, contact may be repeated. Also means *belonging to me*.

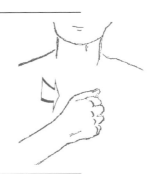

MINICOM

L. 'Y' hand is held above the wiggling fingers of R. hand. A minicom is a type of text 'phone on which messages are typed, displayed, and transmitted down a 'phone line.

MISTAKE, ACCIDENT, SORRY

Clawed hand held near side of head, makes short, quick shaking movements from the wrist. Shoulders may lift slightly.

MORE

R. flat hand taps back of L. hand twice, or R. hand contacts back of L. then moves forwards. Both hands are held with palms facing backwards.

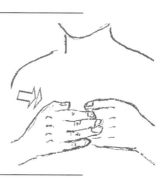

MORNING

R. bent hand with thumb up; finger tips touch left, then right upper chest. Also means **good morning**. May vary regionally.

MOTHER, MUMMY

R. 'M' hand taps L. palm twice. In some regions, 'M' hand taps side of forehead, or back of L. ring finger. Fingerspelt initials 'MF' for *parents*.

MUST, HAVE TO

Palm facing flat hands move sharply down with emphasis. Also means *compulsory* and similar meanings.

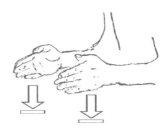

NAME, CALLED

Extended fingers of 'N' hand touch side of forehead, then move away, twisting to palm forward.

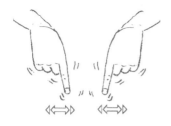

NERVOUS, ANXIOUS
Index fingers point downwards in front of body, and hands make quick shaking/trembling movements from wrists. Can be signed with open hands, or other variations.

NIGHT, DARK
Flat hands held palm back in front of face swing down/in to cross each other. Reversed movement means *day*, *light*.

NORMAL, NATURAL
Extended fingers of R. 'N' hand tap twice on L. palm.

NOT, DON'T

Palm down flat hands start crossed then swing sharply apart as the head shakes. Also means *no*, *not allowed*, *finished*, *forbidden*, *off* and related meanings.

NOT YET, BEFORE

Palm down closed hands make small quick side to side shaking movements in front of body as the head shakes. Also means *wait*, (can be small up and down movements).

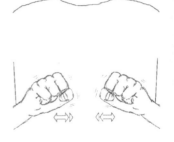

NOTHING, NO-ONE

Palm forward 'O' hand (a full 'O' hand can be used), shakes slightly from side to side, or makes small circles. Both hands can be used. The head shakes.

NOW, TODAY

Flat hands, palms facing up, make short repeated downward movement. One emphatic movement for *at once*, *right now*, *immediately* and similar meanings.

NURSE

Tips of 'C' hand are drawn across the forehead. Other variations include tip of R. thumb or index finger making a cross on left upper arm.

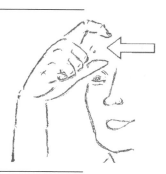

OLD, ELDERLY

'V' hand held palm back in front of nose moves down slightly as extended fingers bend.

OPERATION, SURGERY

R. thumb tip is drawn sharply down L. palm. Can be signed with R. thumb tip drawn across appropriate part of anatomy. Also means *cut*, *scar*, *wound*.

PAIN, SHARP PAIN

Index fingers make short movements towards each other, on appropriate part of anatomy, e.g. *contractions*, *labour pains* located on abdomen.

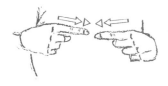

PAIN RELIEF

Thumb extended from closed hand flexes several times (self-administered type). Also used for *push button alarm*.

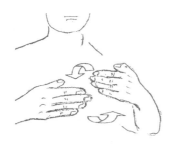

PATIENCE, PATIENT

Flat hands rotate backwards, brushing alternately downwards on body. The lips are pressed together. Also means *calm, endure, tolerate*.

PENIS

Palm up full 'C' hand moves forward in small arc from front of lower abdomen. Can also be indicated by index finger held in same location.

PERHAPS, MAYBE

'Y' hand makes small quick repeated twisting movements from the wrist. The lips may be stretched, and the eyebrows slightly raised.

PERIOD, MENSTRUATION

Hands form repeated fingerspelt initial 'P', or full 'O' hand springs open/down on lower abdomen, or other variations. See also entry for *blood*.

PILL, TABLET

Index finger and thumb flick open near mouth, once for *the pill* (contraceptive pill), repeated for other forms. Full 'O' hand springs open and covers mouth for *overdose*.

PLEASE, IF YOU PLEASE

Tips of flat hand contact chin, then hand moves down/forward as fingers close onto palm. Can be made without final closing movement.

POLICE

Extended fingers of R. 'V' hand flex as they move backwards across back of L. wrist.

PRIVATE, SECRET

Index edge of flat hand taps mouth twice. Also means *in confidence*, and sometimes used to mean *private parts*.

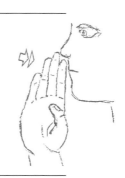

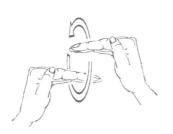

PROCEDURE, PROCESS

Bent hands revolve round each other, moving forwards in front of the body. Also means *get on with*, *ongoing*, *proceed*.

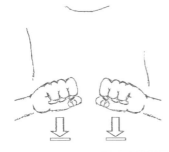

PUSH, BEAR DOWN

Palm down fists make short downward pushing movements. Flat hands may also be used.

QUEASY, NAUSEOUS

Tips of clawed hand rotate on front of body, with appropriate negative expression. Can also be located on stomach. Also means *anxious*, *scared*, *uneasy*, *worried* and similar meanings.

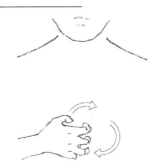

QUESTION, QUERY

'O' hand moves in small circle, then makes short forward movement (outline shape of question mark).

QUICK, EARLY, SUDDEN

R. index finger lands on L. and bounces sharply up. Also means *immediate*, *urgent*.

QUIET, PEACEFUL

'O' hands start in contact, then move apart/down. May start with index finger on the lips and "sh" lip-pattern (*be quiet*).

READ

Fingers of R. 'V' hand, pointing towards L. palm, move from side to side or in direction to suit context (fingers represent direction of eye gaze).

READY, PREPARE
Thumbs of palm down open hands tap chest twice or make small upward brushing movements. Also means *already*.

RELATIONSHIP, BOND
Interlocked 'O' hands move forward and back several times (also means *liaise, relate*). Moved in horizontal circle, means *co-ordinate, unite*).

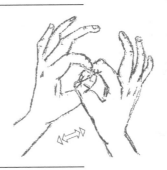

RESIDENTIAL, STAY
Palm in 'C' hands touch temples, then move forward/down, twisting to finish palm down. Flat hands also sometimes used.

RIGHT, CONFIRM

R. closed hand with thumb out, bangs down onto L. palm. The head nods. Also means *accurate*, *correct*, *proper*.

RISK, RISKY

Index and thumb tips of 'O' hand make small tapping movements against front of neck. Lips may be stretched and teeth clenched.

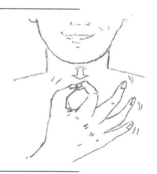

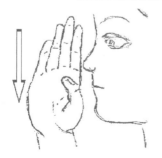

SAD, SERIOUS, SOLEMN

Index edge of flat hand moves slowly down in front of face. The mouth is turned down and brows furrowed.

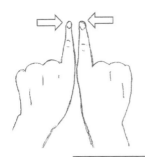

SAME, ALSO, TOO

Index fingers extended and pointing forward, move in to contact each other. Contact may be repeated.

SANITARY TOWEL

Palm down 'C' hands move apart and slightly upwards in outline shape of towel.

SCAN, ULTRASOUND.

Index edge of full 'O' hand moves in circular movements on appropriate part of body. Different types of scan would be signed differently.

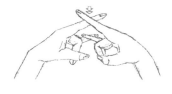

SEX, SEXUAL/ITY

Index and little fingers of both hands extended, R. on top of L. with small repeated contact (based on fingerspelt 'SX' formation). There are a number of different variations.

SEX, INTERCOURSE

Bent hands with thumbs extended bang against each other, so that thumbs interlock. May vary, e.g. palm facing fists make short repeated movements towards each other.

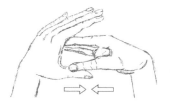

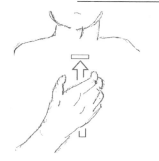

SHOCK, SURPRISE

Tips of hand with fingers curved move sharply up front of chest ending abruptly. Can be signed with palm back open hands on chest moving sharply forward as mouth opens.

SHOWER

Full "O" hand held up and forward moves back/down towards signer's face and head, as fingers spring open several times.

SICK, VOMIT

Open hand brushes up body and forward from mouth. Tips of clawed hand rub stomach in circles for *feel sick*, *queasy*.

SIGN, SIGNATURE

Tips of slightly bent extended fingers of 'N' hand move down to contact L. palm. May be preceded by the sign *name*. Also means *booking*, *contract*. See entry for *write*.

SIGN, SIGN LANGUAGE

Open hands move in alternate forward circles. Hands may rub together, or other small variations, and changes in context.

SIT, SEAT, SIT DOWN

Fingers of R. bent 'V' hand hook over extended fingers of L. 'N' hand or palm down flat hands, one on top of the other, move downwards.

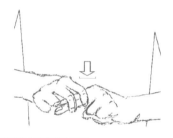

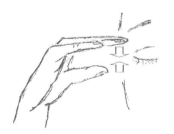

SLEEP, ASLEEP

Fingers close onto thumbs near eyes. Eyes may close with movement. Both hands may be used.

SLOW/LY, AGES, LONG TIME

Fingers of R. flat hand move slowly up left forearm. Index finger is sometimes used.

SMEAR, CERVICAL SMEAR

R. thumb tucked into bent index (Irish T hand, see page 126) moves towards opening of L. full 'C' hand and makes small twisting movements.

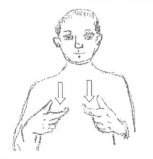

SOCIAL WORKER, WELFARE

Index and thumb tips of 'C' hands move downwards on chest. Movement may be repeated. Fingerspelt 'SW' also sometimes used.

SOME, SEVERAL

Pad of thumb rubs along fingertips from little finger to index.

SOMEONE, WHO?

Upright index finger moves in small horizontal circles. A large sweeping circle means **everyone**. A questioning expression indicates question form in **who?**

SORRY, REGRET

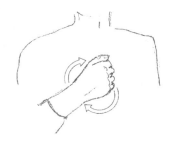

Closed hand rubs in small circles on chest. Little finger may be extended. In some regions a flat hand is used. Also means **apology**. See also **mistake**, **sorry**.

SPECIAL, SPECIALIST

Palm down hands with index fingers pointing forward; R. index brushes sharply forward against L. Can also be signed with 'O' hand making small forward movement.

START, BEGIN

Extended R. thumb brushes sharply down L. palm. Another variation uses palm down open hands snapping sharply shut as they twist up to palm forward.

STAY, STOP THERE

Two 'C' hands with palms facing forward/down, make small firm movement down (can be one hand only). Also means *stay still*. Hands move to the right for *continue*.

STITCHES, NEEDLE

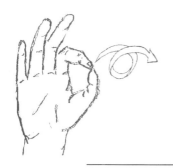

'O' hand makes repeated twisting movements in action of stitching. Can be located on the appropriate part of the anatomy to suit the context.

STOP, WAIT

Palm forward flat hand makes short firm forward movement. Both hands may be used. With repeated movement means *hang on*, *hold on*, *wait*.

STRESS, TENSION

Clawed hands with palms facing inwards move in to contact, one above the other and twist inward in squeezing action on chest. Also means *grief*, *frustration*. May vary.

97

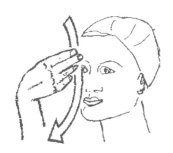

STROKE

Tips of R. bent hand move sharply downwards in front of face.

STRONG, ENERGY

Both hands clench into fists and bend sharply upwards at the elbows, or R. index outlines biceps on left upper arm (also *muscle*).

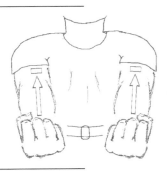

SUBTITLES, CAPTIONS

'C' hands with palms facing forward move apart twice, or palm back clawed hands wiggle, moving side to side. '*888*' is also used to refer to *teletext subtitles*.

SUPPOSITORY, PESSARY

Index and thumb of R. hand move into the 'O' formed by index and thumb of L. hand. R. hand enters from other side for **tampon**, or **vaginal pessary**.

SURE, REAL, TRUE

R. flat hand lands sharply edge down onto L. palm with emphasis. Also means **certain**, **definite**. R. hand rests on L. and wavers slightly, for **uncertain**, **not sure**.

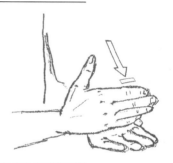

SUSPICIOUS, WARY

Palm down 'Y' hand makes several short movements, forwards, or towards item/person referred to. The eyes are narrowed. Also means **suspect**.

SWALLOW

Index finger moves up to mouth, then twists over to point and move down front of chest.

TEA, CUP, DRINK FROM CUP

'O' hand makes small backward tipping movement towards the mouth. An Irish 'T' hand is also alternatively used.

TELEVISION, TV

Fingerspell 'TV', or index fingers trace outline shape of screen. R. index prods L. palm repeatedly for *remote control,* or *teletext.*

TESTICLES

Index, middle fingers and thumbs of both palm up hands are extended and bent;hands make small alternate up/down circular movements. May vary.

THANK YOU, THANKS

Fingertips of palm back flat hands contact mouth/chin, then move forward/down and apart. Can be one hand only. Also means *grateful*, *thankful*.

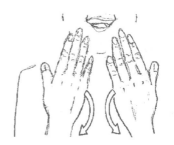

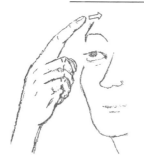

THINK

Index finger touches side of forehead (taps twice for *sensible*). May make small circular movements, also meaning *mull over*, *ponder* and similar meanings.

THIRSTY, DRY

Fingers and thumb held on throat, hand moves forward/down as fingers close onto thumb, or index finger brushes down on throat As drawn, also means *fancy*, *wish*.

TIME, WHAT TIME?

R. extended index taps back of L. wrist several times. A questioning expression indicates question form.

TIRED, EXHAUSTED

Little fingers extended and twisted back to touch body, move slowly down body. Head may be tilted to one side and the cheeks puffed out. May vary.

TOILET

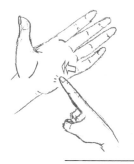

Index finger of R. hand taps against L. hand in repeated fingerspelt 'T' formation. There are a number of variations, but this version is commonly understood.

TOMORROW, NEXT DAY

Extended index finger swings forward/down from side of cheek to finish palm up.

TOSS AND TURN

Fingers of R. 'V' hand contact L. palm and twist over and back several times (used here as legs classifier). Also means *restless*.

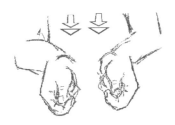

TREAT, TREATMENT
Palm facing closed hands with thumbs tucked into bent index fingers, make short repeated forward movements. May change direction in context.

TROUBLE, BOTHER
Tips of right bent hand tap back of L. hand twice. Also means *naughty, nuisance*. R. hand makes single contact then moves off twisting to palm up for *not bothered*.

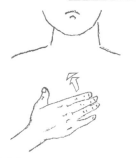

UPSET, DISTRESSED
Flat hand makes small repeated upward brushing movements on the chest. With a single downward movement, the meaning is *calm, quiet*.

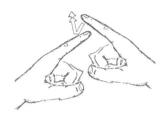

URGENT, FAST, QUICK

R. index contacts L. and bounces sharply back up (face/body express urgency). Also means **early**, **sudden**. Quick repeated taps for **hurry**, **emergency**.

URINE, URINATE

Index finger flicks downwards off thumb several times in front of lower abdomen. May vary. Used with lip-pattern **pee, wee,** or with sound/lip-pattern "pssss."

USE, USEFUL

Tip of thumb makes small repeated downward brushing movement on chin. Fingertips of bent hand also sometimes alternatively used in some regions.

VAGINA, VULVA

Tips of extended index fingers and thumbs tap together twice, pointing down in front of lower abdomen.

WAIT, HANG ON

Palm down bent hands (or closed hands) make two small movements down in front of body. Can also be signed by flat hand held palm forward with small repeated movement.

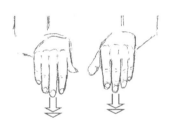

WAKE UP, AWAKE, AWARE

Index finger and thumb flick open at side of eye. Both hands can be used.

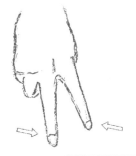

WALK, WALKING

Fingers of 'V' hand pointing down, wiggle as hand moves forward. Can also be signed with palm down flat hands moving in forward 'steps' alternately, or other variations.

WANT, NEED, WISH

Open hand brushes down side of body in small movement, twisting to palm down A flat hand may also be used.

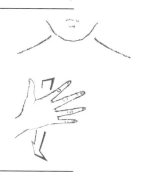

WARM

Clawed hand held palm back in front of mouth, makes small circular movements. A sharp movement to the right across the mouth means **hot**.

WEAK, FEEBLE

Edge of extended R. little finger moves down left upper arm. Can be signed by tip of index finger twisting into cheek, or palm down open hands flop over to palm up.

WEIGH, WEIGHT

Palm up flat hands move alternately up and down in front of body. Also means *assess, compare*, and words of similar meanings.

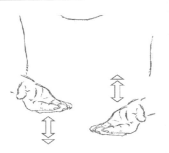

WELL, FIT, HEALTHY

Tips of bent hands contact chest, then hands move forward and close with thumbs up. Also a common greeting sign, e.g. "*how are you?*" with raised eyebrows.

WET, DAMP, MOIST

Palm up bent hand opens and closes onto ball of thumb twice (both hands may be used). Thumb rubs across pads of fingers for *dry, dried up*.

WHAT? WHAT FOR?

Palm forward extended index finger shakes side to side in short quick movements. Face and body show questioning expression.

WHEN? WHAT TIME?

Fingertips of open hand wiggle against side of cheek repeatedly. face and body show questioning expression.

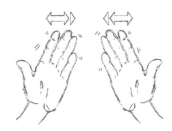

WHERE?

Palm up flat hands make small repeated movements towards each other, or make small inward circular movements. Face and body show questioning expression.

WHICH? EITHER

Palm down 'Y' hand moves side to side or between items or people referred to. May change direction in context. Face and body show question form in *which?*

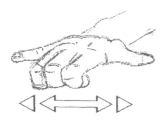

WHY? BECAUSE, REASON

Edge of R. index finger taps left side of upper chest twice. Face and body show question form as in *why? what reason?* and so on.

WILL, WOULD, SHALL

Palm forward closed hand twists to palm down on side of cheek. Can be signed with index tip on cheek twisting in same movement (regional).

WIND, FLATULENCE

Tips of clawed hand move in small circles on abdomen. Face indicates discomfort. Located on chest, also used to describe general *discomfort, unease*, or *worry*.

WINDOW

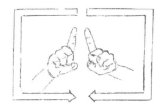

Index fingers move in outline shape. Also used to indicate outline shape of many different objects e.g. *monitor, screen, sheet of paper*, and so on.

WON'T, REFUSE

Fingers flexed behind thumb spring sharply open in small forward movement from side of cheek. The head shakes.

WORK/ER, JOB

Little finger edge of R. flat hand chops down twice onto index edge of L. flat hand at right angles. If cheeks are puffed, means *busy*, *hard work*.

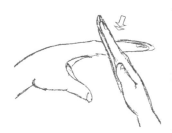

WORRY, CONCERN

Clawed hand held near side of head twists sharply down from wrist in front of the face. Both hands can be used. The brows are furrowed.

WORSE, WORSEN

Tip of extended R. little finger brushes down against tip of L. little finger twice. Fingers may start crossed and pull slowly down/apart The brows may be furrowed.

WRITE, SIGN FOR

Closed hand with index and thumb tip touching moves to the right in wiggling movement. Also means *notes, office, signature*.

WRONG, FAULT

Edge of R. little finger taps L. palm twice. With raised eyebrows means *what's wrong?* If R. hand moves in circular movement, the meaning is *rotten, poor, shoddy*.

X-RAY

Repeated fingerspelt 'X', or full fingerspelt 'XRAY' may be used.

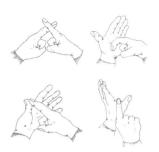

YESTERDAY, DAY BEFORE

Extended index finger, palm back, touches side of chin, then drops down/back, or moves to point back over shoulder.

YOUNG, YOUTH

Fingers of 'N' hand move forward and close onto thumb in front of nose, or repeated fingerspelt initial 'Y'. May vary regionally.

YOU, HE, SHE, IT

Index finger points forward or towards person concerned. Point back to self for *I, me*. Also means *that*. (Pointing is not considered rude in the deaf community).

YOUR/S, HIS, HER

Palm forward closed hand makes small forward movement, or towards person concerned.

SIGN INVENTION:
CLASSIFYING HANDSHAPES
The DIY, Self-Assembly Flat-Pack Section

SIGN INVENTION

The DIY, Self-Assembly Flat-Pack Section

Sign language learners frequently ask the question "what is the sign for ... " and, because of their experience of spoken languages, constantly look for word equivalents in BSL. However, as described in the **Introduction**, sign languages tend to be more flexible, inventive and less word based than spoken languages, allowing users to create signs on the spot, as they are needed. This is not just random mime and gesture, but involves consistent use of the building blocks of BSL to produce meaningful combinations that may be unique to that situation and never used before.

This process has been termed the do-it-yourself or **DIY lexicon**, and is explained in the BSL/English dictionary as follows;

> *"However, there is another major category of BSL vocabulary which the native signer manipulates with consummate ease and which the learner must clue into if s/he is ever to make full sense of the language. This is what has been called the **productive lexicon** ... The signer, in a sense creates words as they are needed and in doing so may produce combinations which have never actually been used before, but which are fully understandable and meaningful in context ... "*

This section of the book functions as a **DIY 'flat-pack'**, since it contains some basic components, with simple instructions of assembly, and it can be easily transported.

As with all flat-packs, there will be bits missing and you may need to enlist the help of others to help you understand it and bring it all together, but once mastered, even if a bit wobbly, it will be something you have constructed for yourself.

It is useful therefore both from a practical point of view and also a language learning standpoint, to look at some of the building blocks that may be particularly useful in medical settings that can be implemented to suit the communication needs of the moment.

There are certain handshapes that will crop up again and again in medical settings and the following are an attempt to pull out the most useful and productive.

Deaf people's way of relating to the world involves a visuality – a different conceptual base that hearing people may not be used to and need to clue into. Signs created by Deaf people in this way are more often based on what actions or objects look like or are used for than by name.

This section of the book is concerned with handshapes that function as **CLASSIFIERS**. They can be used to refer to actions and objects based on their physical shape or outline, or how they are grasped, handled and moved. There are over 40 handshapes identified as classifiers. There are just 6 selected here as being particularly relevant for health care settings and which should give the basic idea.

A comprehensive description of the DIY lexicon, classifying handshapes and other details of BSL grammar are given in the British Deaf Association's BSL/English dictionary (see **Sources and Recommended Reading** at the back of this book).

THE 'O' HAND

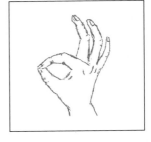

The 'O' hand illustrated here can be used in a number of different ways, particularly in referring to the handling of small delicate objects, for example, *labstix*, *needle*, *stitches*, *thermometer*. It is useful in referring to small round things such as **small hole, stoma**, where the hand can be located on the part of the body relative to the particular context.

Some signs may involve two 'O' hands and are useful for tracing the position of a **catheter** for example, or other devices of similar size, such as a **drip tube**. Instruments with a circular or cylindrical component can also be referred to with this handshape located and moving in an appropriate manner, **stethoscope** and **eyeglass** are two examples.

Many more signs can be created in this way. The location and movements relevant to these meanings are described in more detail on the following pages, along with a number of other **established** signs using this handshape which should also prove helpful in patient care.

ACUPUNCTURE

Tips of 'O' hand (or both hands) make repeated contact with different parts of the body.

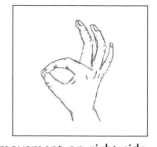

ADVANTAGE, BENEFIT

Index and thumb tips of palm down 'O' hand make small downward brushing movement on right side of upper chest.

CATHETER, NARROW TUBE, RYLES TUBE

Index and thumb tips of 'O' hands contact each other; hands pull apart (directional). Can be one hand only moving in direction tube is to be used e.g. up the nose, urethra and so on.

DEFER, DELAY, POSTPONE, PUT OFF

'O' hands palms down or palms facing, move forward in small arc.

EXACT, PERFECT, PRECISE

Palm left R. 'O' hand makes short abrupt forward/down movement in front of body, lips are stretched and eyes narrowed.

FLESH, SKIN

Palm down 'O' hand pinches back of L. hand and makes short movements side to side holding skin of L. hand.

MEDICAL, DOCTOR

Thumb and index finger edge of 'O hand touches right, then left side of chest. There are a number of variations of this sign (see *stethoscope*).

OVARY, OVARIES

Finger and thumb of 'O' hand (or both hands) are held against side of lower abdomen.

PEE (male)

Palm forward 'O' hand is held on lower abdomen.

SHEETS

'O' hands move up body, palm back, or move in direction to suit context, e.g. in action of pulling sheet across bed.

SPECIAL, SPECIALIST

Palm forward 'O' hand makes two short forward movements. Both hands can be used. Also means *formal* if used in a different context.

STETHOSCOPE, MEDICAL

Tips of 'O' hand touch right then left side of upper chest. Can be signed with both 'O' hands touching ears, then moving forward and together, so that they finish palm forward and touching.

STOCKINGS

Palm back 'O' hands move upwards on upper leg. For **surgical stockings**, fists make hard pulling motion on upper leg, followed by **white** (tips of 'O' hand make small downward brushing  movements on side of upper chest).

SWAP, REPLACE, SUBSTITUTE

'O' hands with palms facing inwards, one held near body, and the other held forward; hands swap places. Hands may start side by side and swap sideways across each other.

SWITCH ON, SWITCH OFF

'O' hand makes small twisting movement from wrist, upwards or downwards.

TABLET, CAPSULE, PILL

Tips of R. 'O' hand contact palm up L. flat hand, then move up to mouth.

THERMOMETER

'O hand makes short movement forward from mouth or makes small shaking movements.

IRISH T HAND

The hand illustrated here, with the thumb tucked into the bent index, is also sometimes known as the Irish T, as it represents the letter 'T' in the Irish fingerspelling alphabet, and this provides a convenient label. This handshape can be used to refer to narrow cylindrically shaped objects or instruments by the way they are handled and used, such as **auriscope** (**otoscope**), **opthalmoscope**, **curette** and so on. It is useful in referring to small objects or those needing fine control, such as **key, razor, shave**, and for flat narrow objects such at **comb**, **spatula**, **toothbrush** and so on.

The Irish 'T' hand, like the 'O' hand, occurs in many established signs which should also prove helpful in patient care, some of which are described here.

ALMOST, NEARLY
Palm back Irish 'T' hand makes two small forward movements. Eyes are narrowed, shoulders hunched.

BRING, FETCH
Palm up Irish 'T' hands move back/left in small arc.

BRUSH TEETH, TOOTHBRUSH

Palm back R. Irish 'T' hand pointing left makes small up/down or side to side movements near mouth.

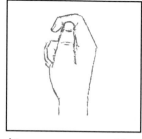

CHEEK, CHEEKY

Cheek is grasped by Irish 'T' hand. May make small shaking movement. Also means *bare*, *naked*.

COMB, COMB HAIR

Palm left R. Irish 'T' hand makes small downward movements near side of head.

COMIC, MAGAZINE, NEWSPAPER

Palm facing Irish 'T' hands twist to palm up as they move apart.

CONTROL, MANAGE, RUN

Palm up Irish 'T' hands make small alternate backwards/forwards movements.

COOK, WHISK

Palm back R. Irish 'T' hand makes small quick circular movements in crook of left arm.

DRESSING GOWN, BATHROBE

Irish 'T' hands twist round each other at side of waist in action of tying cord.

DENTIST, EXTRACTION

Palm left R. Irish 'T' hand makes short sharp downward movement near mouth.

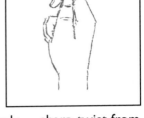

KEY, LOCK

Palm left R. Irish 'T' hand makes quick twisting movements from wrist. A single sharp twist from the wrist can be used for **lock**, **unlock**.

PROSTITUTE, PROSTITUTION

Palm left R. Irish 'T' hand twists to palm back as it makes small movement to the left over left shoulder.

SHAVE, RAZOR

Index edge of Irish 'T' hand brushes twice down cheek, or can be located on body to suit context.

SPOON, EAT WITH SPOON

Irish 'T' hand twists from palm down to palm back in repeated movement towards mouth. Also means **cereal**, **pudding**, **soup**.

SUCCESS, ACHIEVE

Palm left R. Irish 'T' hand pointing up makes small repeated circles at head height.

THE 'GOOD' HAND

A closed hand with thumb extended as illustrated here can be easily recognised for its positive conventional association, and is often the basis of signs with pleasant or

agreeable connotations as can be seen in the illustrated lexicon for signs such as **agree**, **better**, and **right**.

It is also a classifying handshape which is a useful handling and instrumental classifier for instruments with blades, such as **scalpel** with associated additional meanings, such as **cut**, **scar**, **surgery**, **wound** in which the tip of the thumb is drawn across the appropriate part of the body, or, in the case of **circumcision**, is drawn round the tip of the extended L. index finger which is being used as a classifier for long narrow objects, in this case the **penis**.

The good hand occurs in many established signs which should also prove helpful in patient care, some of which are described here.

APPETISING, LOVELY, NICE
Thumb tip of 'good' hand is drawn left to right across the chin.

BELL PRESS
Closed hand with thumb extended; thumb pushes forwards, or flexes.

CIRCUMCISION
Tip of R. extended thumb makes small circles around the tip of extended L. index finger (classifier indicating *penis*).

CLEVER, WISE
R. thumb tip is drawn right to left across forehead.

CONGRATULATE, PRAISE
Closed hands with thumbs up make alternate forward circular movements. May move backwards brushing down chest for *pride, proud*.

CORRECT, PROPER, RIGHT
R. 'good' hand rests palm down on L. palm.

GAY, HOMOSEXUAL
Closed hand with thumb up rests on L. palm and makes short, quick, repeated twisting movements from the wrist. With index finger also extended, means *lesbian*.

NEXT, NEIGHBOUR
Palm down closed hand with thumb extended twists over to finish palm up.

EXTENDED INDEX

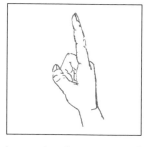

A closed hand with index finger extended as illustrated here provides the basis of many signs, and is particularly useful as a person classifier, where its use, normally in an upright position, can be used to show the location and movement of individual people.

It is also useful as a size and shape specifier for long thin objects, including parts of the body, e.g. **leg**, normally pointing down (two hands for **legs**), and **penis**, located in front of lower abdomen, can be pointing down or upright. The sign **nervous** in the illustrated lexicon is an example of the index fingers used as legs classifiers, representing the legs shaking.

Both index fingers can also be used to draw the outline of an object's size and shape, in the location relevant to the particular context as in **screen**, **monitor**, **TV**, **notice board**, **sign**, **poster**, **window**, **form**, **sheet of paper** and so on. It is also a touch classifier appropriate to actions of the extended index finger, e.g. **prod**, **poke**, **press buttons** (such as TV /Teletext remote, or telephone key pad). Finally, and importantly, the extended index finger is used for pointing to people and things being referred to. Such pointing is not considered rude in Deaf culture.

131

This handshape occurs in many established signs which should also prove helpful in patient care, some of which are described here.

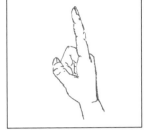

AIDS, HIV
L. 'V' hand is held with the fingers pointing down; extended R. index is held across the back of L. fingers to form a large A shape. *HIV* is usually fingerspelt.

ALARM, (e.g. CLOCK) BELL
R. index held upright, palm facing forward; side of R. index bangs twice against palm of L flat hand, palm facing right.

ALSO, LIKE, SAME
Both hands palms down with index fingers extended and pointing forward, tap together twice. For *different*, hands move apart from this position, twisting to palm up.

BOSS, CHIEF, HEAD
Extended index pointing forward twists sharply to point up at head height. Both hands may be used. Also means *authority*, *in charge*, *manager*, and *God*.

COME, GO

Upright extended index held slightly forward, moves towards signer, palm back. Hand starts near signer and moves away, palm forward, for *go*, *go away*.

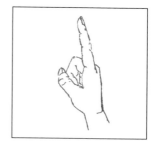

CRUEL, HARSH

R. index finger twists firmly into neck, from palm left to palm back. Also means *kill* (may just prod into side of neck, also meaning *meat*).

DECIDE, DECISION

Inside edge of R. extended index bangs sharply on palm of L. hand. If movement is repeated, as R. hand moves down left arm, the meaning is *policy*, *rules*.

EASY, GENTLY, SIMPLE, SOFT

Tip of extended index prods the cheek twice. Also a regional sign for *period* (menstrual).

EMERGENCY, FAST, HURRY

R. extended index finger, pointing forward/left bounces sharply off end of L. extended index finger pointing forward/right several times.

EYE, EAR, NOSE, THROAT

Index finger points to relevant parts of the anatomy. *'ENT'* is usually fingerspelt. If the index taps the front of the nose twice, the meaning is *nosy*. If the index brushes upwards off the tip of the nose, the meaning is *posh*.

HE, HER, HIM, IT, SHE, YOU, THAT, THIS

Index points in direction of person or object being referred to. Hand sweeps sideways to indicate plural.

IGNORE

Tip of extended index touches ear, then twists sharply to point downwards. Both hands may be used. Also means *take no notice*.

ILL, ILLNESS, POORLY

Extended R. index touches forehead, then moves down to tap against side of extended L. which is pointing forward. There are a number of variations (see illustrated *ill*).

LATE, LATER, HOUR

R. index held upright, palm forward, is held against the palm of L. flat hand which faces left. R. hand twists sharply to point forward/down (*late*). R. hand makes a slower, forward movement for

later, or rotates in a full circle for *hour*.

LOOK, SEE

Index (or 'V' hand) moves forward from near eye.

MEET, FACE TO FACE

Upright index fingers, held apart, with palms facing in towards each other, move towards each other.

NEGATIVE

Outside edge of R. extended index, pointing left, taps against palm forward L. palm.

NOISE, NOISY, LOUD

Index finger pointing in towards the ear, moves in small forward circles.

POSITIVE

Extended index fingers contact each other, twice, in the form a cross, or plus sign.

ROOM, WARD
Index fingers pointing down move in outline shape of a square.

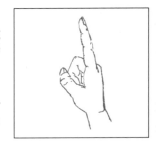

SAY, TELL
Extended index finger moves forward from mouth.

SHY, BASHFUL
Tip of extended index finger on chin; hand twists from palm left to palm back.

TEMPERATURE
L. extended index held upright; R. extended index held across it in form of plus sign, makes short movements up and down.

REBUKE, TELL OFF, WARN
Upright R. index finger with palm facing left, shakes forward several times. The brows are furrowed.

BENT 'V' HAND

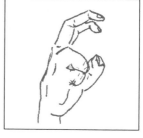

A bent 'V' hand, with the index and middle fingers extended and bent, as illustrated here is not one of the most common handshapes, but is worth a mention as it is particularly useful as a legs classifier (often palm down), showing location and movement in highly productive ways, (*sit* in the illustrated section is one example of this), and in signs such as *climbing stairs* (the fingers wiggle as the hand moves diagonally upwards).

It is also used to indicate removal of small things, so is particularly useful for procedures such as *adenoidectomy*, *appendicectomy* and *tonsillectomy* for example, in which the palm faces backwards and the backs of the extended bent fingers move forward from the appropriate area of the anatomy. *Lumpectomy* may also fall into this category, although it is more usually signed with the thumb also extended and bent.

Some other useful established signs using a bent 'V' hand are described on the following page.

BATTERY, ELECTRIC
Extended fingertips of bent 'V' hand tap twice against chin.

BLIND, BLIND PERSON
Bent 'V' hand held with palm facing backwards makes short repeated side to side movements in front of eyes.

FAECES, SHIT
Extended fingertips of bent 'V' hand make short movement downwards on the side of the face.

GET OFF, ALIGHT, DROP (someone) OFF
Palm down bent 'V' hand moves forward or to the side in small arc with small twisting movement, off L. hand.

IMPLANT
Extended fingertips of bent 'V' hand contact the appropriate part of the anatomy with emphasis.

WALK, WALKING
Extended fingertips of bent 'V' hand brush forwards repeatedly on L. flat hand, palm up, or can be located and move in a manner appropriate to the context.

FLAT HAND

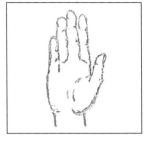

Finally in this section of useful handshapes, is the FLAT hand shown here. The flat hand is useful as a vehicle classifier, and can show the position/shape of vehicles, appearing in such signs as *traffic queue* and *car park* (not illustrated). It is useful for referring to objects with flat surfaces, e.g. *book*, *door*, *table*, *wall* and for flat instruments, e.g. *saw*, with associated meanings such as *amputate*, in which it would be located on the appropriate part of the body. It is also useful for tracing the position and size of objects with flat or smooth surfaces, such as *basin*, *vase*.

Some other useful established signs using the flat hand are described here.

ACCESS, INTERRUPT, INTERVENE
Palm left R. flat hand, pointing forward moves forward to pass between fingers of palm back L. flat hand.

AIR, COOL
Palm back flat hands held in front and to sides of face, waft backwards several times. Also means *weather*.

ALL, EVERY, EVERYONE

R. flat hand, palm forward/down sweeps left in a horizontal arc.

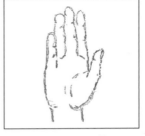

AMPUTATE, CUT OFF

Little finger edge of flat hand in drawn in slicing movement across appropriate part of the anatomy. Breast amputation (**mastectomy**) can be signed with the thumb tip of the 'good' hand drawn under and around the breast area.

ANYWAY, NEVER MIND, SORT OUT

Palm back flat hands with fingers pointing inwards, brush alternately backwards and forwards so that fingertips brush against each other.

ADULT, GROWN UP

Flat hand is held at head height, palm down.

BREATHE, PANT

Flat hand held on upper chest moves backwards and forwards slowly several times for **breathe**, or quickly and with exaggeration for **pant**.

CLAIM

Palm back flat hand, fingers pointing up moves firmly forward/down to finish palm up.

CONTENT, SATISFIED

Palm down flat hand makes small downward brushing movement on upper chest, with appropriate facial expression. Single movement down with air blown through lips means *relief*.

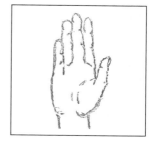

DOUBT, MAYBE

Palm up flat hands move alternately up and down, lips are pressed together and head slightly tilted.

END, FINAL, LAST

Palm back R. flat hand with fingers pointing left lands edge down on to extended L. little finger.

EXCUSE, APOLOGISE, FORGIVE

Tips of R. flat hand touch lips then move down to rub in small circular movements on L. palm.

EXPLAIN, TELL ABOUT

Palm up flat hands with fingers pointing inwards rotate round each other in forward movement (*I'll explain*) or rotate backwards towards signer (*explain to me*). Directional.

FLANNEL, WASH
Palm back flat hand in front of face moves round in small circles. Can be located on appropriate part of body.

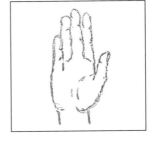

HEART
Palm back flat hands taps left upper chest twice.

HEREDITARY, PASSED ON
Palm up flat hand held at shoulder height in front of body with fingers pointing forward. Hand moves down/left in small steps. May start from left shoulder moving forward/down in small steps.

HOSPITAL
Palm facing flat hands held a few inches apart, with fingers pointing forwards, make small forward circles simultaneously. See also illustrated section.

LUCKY FORTUNATE
Palm left R. flat hand pointing up near side of head makes short backward/forward shaking movements.

MEAN, MEANING
Fingers of palm down R. flat hand rub palm of L. flat hand in small circles.

NEVER

R. flat hand brushes sharply down past the back of L. flat hand.

PERIOD (MENSTRUAL)

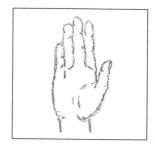

Index finger edge of upright R. flat hand, palm facing left, taps twice against lips. Also means *private*.

PSYCHOLOGY

Little finger edge of palm left R. flat hand taps the space between back of L. thumb and index finger.

SATISFIED, CONTENT

Index finger edge of palm down flat hand makes short repeated downward brushing movements on upper chest. Single slow movement as air is blown through lips also means *relief*.

SUNDAY, CHURCH, PRAY

Upright flat hands tap together twice. If the hands are held together and make several short movements forward, the meaning is *religion*.

THIRSTY, WATER

Tips of palm back flat hand brush down throat twice.

FINGERSPELLING

Some countries of the world use a one-handed manual alphabet, but Britain, and a handful of other countries, use the two-handed system illustrated opposite. Fingerspelling represents the letters of the alphabet, and although an integrated and important part of BSL, its use varies considerably between individuals, according to the situation, or because of regional and educational influences.

Since it is a direct representation of English words, it should be used with caution, but it still has a significant role as a bridge to communication.

Older people and people in the North of England and Scotland tend to use more fingerspelling in all contexts than younger people and those in the South. Fingerspelling can be used for full English words (e.g. *staff, cancer*), for names and places, and also for acronyms, like *ENT, HIV, HRT, NHS.*

Abbreviations are also common, for example *January* – 'JAN', *Monday* – 'MON' and repeated initial letters such as *mothe*r – 'MM' and *natural* 'NN'. Practice is needed for fluent patterns, but when the letters merge, they appear quite different to their static, drawn image, so that regularly spelt small words like *DAY*, *IF*, and *SON* are recognised as 'signs'.

BRITISH TWO-HANDED FINGERSPELLING ALPHABET

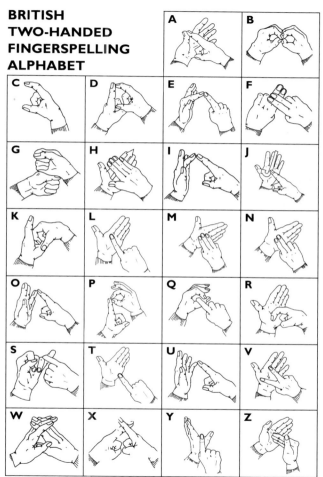

Illustrations by Joanne Dunn

SOURCES AND RECOMMENDED READING

British Deaf Association (1992). *Dictionary of British Sign Language/English.* London: Faber and Faber.

Collins, Judith M. (1994). *Who Needs Medical Interpreters?* Issues in Interpreting Conference April 1994 (unpublished).

Collins, Judith M. (1996). *Medical Stress – Deaf Women as Patients.* Deaf Worlds, Issue 1, Volume 12, 1996.

Centre for Deaf Studies University of Bristol Research notes 1: *Language Development in School.*

Centre for Deaf Studies University of Bristol Research Notes 9: *The Manual Alphabet in BSL.*

Deaf Professionals in Mental Health (1997). *Sign Language in Mental Health.* British Society for Mental Health and Deafness.

Smith, C. (2005). *Let's Sign Pocket Dictionary: BSL Concise Beginner's Guide.* Stockton on Tees: Co-Sign Communications.

Smith, C. (2009). *Let's Sign Dictionary: Everyday BSL for Learners* 2nd Edition Revised & Updated. Stockton on Tees: Co-Sign Communications.

The Royal National Institute for Deaf People (1999). *Breaking the Sound Barrier. Can You Hear Us?* Deaf people's experience of social exclusion, isolation and prejudice. London: RNID.

USEFUL ADDRESSES

Numbers for voice contact are indicated by (V)
and for text contact by (T)

British Association of Teachers of the Deaf (BATOD)
Paul Simpson, Secretary
e-mail: secretary@batod.org.uk
web: www.batod.org.uk

British Deaf Association (BDA)
Coventry Point 10th Floor, Market Way,
Coventry CV1 1EA.
Tel/Voice: 02476 550936
Tel/Text: 02476 550393
Fax: 02476 221541
e-mail: headoffice@bda.org.uk
web: www.bda.org.uk

SIGNATURE
Mersey House
Mandale Business Park
Belmont
Durham DH1 1TH
Tel: 0191 383 1155 (V/T)
Text: 0191 383 7915   **Fax:** 0191 383 7914
e-mail: durham@signature.org.uk
web: www.signature.org.uk

DEAFSIGN
Incorporating DeafBooks.co.uk
(For *Let's Sign* BSL Resources)
16 Highfield Crescent, Hartburn,
Stockton on Tees TS18 5HH.
Tel: 01642 580505 (V/T)
e-mail: cath@deafsign.com
web: www.deafsign.com
LET'S SIGN Series
web: www.DeafBooks.co.uk

Forest Books
The New Building, Ellwood Road, Milkwall,
Coleford,
Gloucestershire GL16 7LE.
Tel: 01594 833858 (V/T)
Videophone: 01594 810637
Fax: 01594 833446
e-mail: forest@forestbooks.com
web: www.ForestBooks.com

**The National Deaf Children's Society
(NDCS)**
National Office, 15 Dufferin Street,
London EC1Y 8UR.
Freephone Helpline:
Mon-Fri 10am - 5pm 0808 800 8880 (V/T)
Fax: 020 7251 5020
Switchboard Tel: 020 7490 8656 (V/T)
e-mail: helpline@ndcs.org.uk
web: www.ndcs.org.uk

RNID
19-23 Featherstone Street,
London EC1Y 8SL.
Information line:
Tel: 0808 808 0123 (freephone)
Textphone: 0808 808 9000 (freephone)
e-mail: informationline@rnid.org.uk
web: www.rnid.org.uk

Sign Health
5 Baring Road, Beaconsfield,
Buckinghamshire, HP9 2NB
Tel: 01494 687600
Textphone: 01494 687626
e-mail: info@signhealth.org.uk
web: www.signhealth.org.uk

Useful websites with free video sign material for learners

www.signstation.org
www.signedstories.com
www.slcresources4ict.net

www.signpostbsl.com
www.ndcshandsup.org
www.deafparent.org.uk

www.britishsignlanguage.com
www.sciencesigns.ac.uk/home_glossary.asp
www.ssc.education.ed.ac.uk/bsl/list.html
www.radlegalservices.org.uk

INDEX

D

157

S

160